"You've gotta have a sense of humor about being a woman. That's why they invented bad hair days. And that's why Jan's books are so funny. She's been a frequent guest on my show because her wonderful humor hits us right in the funny bone."

Jenny Jones
"Jenny Jones Show" – NBC

• • •

"Jan King's words are wisdom delivered with humor and style. They should not be missed!"

John Kelly and Marilyn Turner
"Company Show" – WXYZ TV - Detroit

OTHER TITLES BY JAN KING

HORMONES FROM HELL
(The Ultimate <u>Women's</u> Humor Book!)

•

HUSBANDS FROM HELL

•

IT'S BETTER TO BE OVER THE HILL–THAN UNDER IT

KILLER BRAS

And Other Hazards Of The Fifties

by
JAN KING

Illustrated by DON SMITH

Published by

CCC Publications
21630 Lassen Street
Chatsworth, CA 91311

Copyright © 1993 Jan King

Manufactured in the United States Of America

Cover © 1993 CCC Publications

Interior illustrations © 1993 CCC Publications

Cover & Interior art by Don Smith

Interior layout & production by Oasis Graphics

Back cover wardrobe courtesy of Karen Dasesh and Linda Wexler

ISBN: 0-918259-50-9

If your local U.S. bookstore is out of stock, copies of this book may be obtained by mailing check or money order for $5.95 per book (plus $2.50 to cover postage and handling) to: CCC Publications; 21630 Lassen St.; Chatsworth, CA 91311.

Pre-publication Edition - 7/93
First Printing - 10/93

DEDICATION

This book is dedicated with love and pride
to the best production of my life
my two sons
Michael and Philip King.

CONTENTS

INTRODUCTION

Remember when cars looked like phallic symbols and girls were afraid to touch them? Did this exemplify the typical mind set of the fifties or what?? "Nice" girls never discussed sex— it was simply too gross to think that your parents were still *doing it,* much less that someday we'd be *doing it,* too. We were afraid that if we even THOUGHT about what an orgasm felt like, it would raise zits on our faces the size of cheese pizzas.

Those were the days when saying the word "condom" was like saying the "F" word. And according to the magazine ads, we should only WHISPER the word "Kotex." God only knows what would've happened if we shouted it. And those girls who had enough nerve to actually insert a tampon were labeled "experienced" and "fast."

Guilt and *fear* were a way of life for all teens in the fifties. If you weren't feeling both of these emotions at all times, your life was nowhere. All of us teenagers were never without the following catastrophes weighing heavily on our minds:

a. we could be vaporized by the A-bomb at any time

b. someone in our family might be fingered as a "Commie"

c. we were doomed to hell because we French-kissed a boy on our last date.

But one thing was for sure— the fashions of the fifties were about the **worst** in all of recorded time. All of us gals looked like cookie-cutter mannequins in our "poodle" skirts, cardigan sweater sets with the lace collar attached, ballerina flats, and chiffon scarves tied around our pony tails. And underneath it all, we wore starched crinolines, nylon hose with seams running up the back, garter belts, and circular stitched bras that came to saber points.

It's really ironic that nowadays, the kids have "eighty-sixed" the skirts and sweaters but still wear the exact same underwear— only now it's **worn on the outside.**

"KILLER BRAS" is going to take you on a nostalgic trip back to the "Fabulous Fifties" and resurrect those fond and not-so-fond memories of your high school proms, heart-throb dates, beehive hairdos, strangulating girdles, pancake make-up and more. And the guys are not forgotten, either. From the memories of being a duck-tailed greaser to buying your first condom, "KILLER BRAS" dares to go where all men have gone before.

CHAPTER 1

BRAS OF THE FIFTIES: A TRIP DOWN MAMMARY LANE

MAMMARY MANIA: A SWELL ERA

In the fifties, Hollywood elevated the boob to it's rightful place in history. Marilyn Monroe, Jayne Mansfield, Jane Russell, Gina Lollabrigida, Anita Ekberg, and Diana Dors collectively possessed more mammary tissue than the rest of the world's population combined. We could never be called an "underdeveloped nation"—that's for sure. And all that glandular tissue was pushed, squeezed, and molded to fill out some of the most torturous bras ever invented for that era.

This mammary craze had all of us teenage girls ordering the Mark Eden bust developers by the carload in the hopes that we could raise even about 1/10 the size of a Hollywood breast on our puny chests. And even though they often failed to fill our expectations and our cups, we could always rely on the Kleenex factories working double shifts to keep the teenage bras of America bulging at all times.

95% OF THE WORLD'S MAMMARY TISSUE
WAS FOUND IN HOLLYWOOD

BRA CONSTRUCTION: MAKING MOUNTAINS OUT OF MOLEHILLS

Here are a few of the popular bras of the times which magically transformed our AAA cups into the illusion of mounds of C cup flesh. Many of these, like the one made for Jane Russell in "The Outlaw," were pioneered at the Howard Hughes Germ Free Aerodynamic Laboratory just north of the Vegas Strip. And even though many of the prototypes became airborne and flew off shortly after they were made, there were still these classic few which have survived down to the present day.

THE MERRY WIDOW: These were made from 50 gauge all-weather tarpaulin canvas and reinforced with genuine whalebones procured from Moby Dick, himself. The Merry Widow had the amazing capability of molding even the plumpest of teenage figures into a perfect hourglass silhouette under prom gowns.

However, they could not be worn for long periods of time before we gals suffered some pretty major side effects. Many girls sustained fractured ribs and became woozy from oxygen deprivation about an hour into their dates. In this hypoxic state, our moral resolve was severely compromised and we literally turned to "putty" in our dates' hands. And if those hands were dexterous enough to unfasten 76 sets of stainless steel bra hooks before you arrived home, he ended up with a lot more than putty in them. Let's just say we had a lot "riding" on that ride home.

3

THE ORIGINAL "LIVING" BRA

The Merry Widow bra also had some unusual moves of it's own on the dance floor. Utmost caution had to be taken during those tricky underarm spins, because the bra remained steadfastly cinched to the waist and acted as a launching pad, propelling your cleavage upward at full warp speed. This made it possible to knock yourself out in more ways than one doing the shag. Plus, these bras were so intractable, when you did the Cha-Cha, your bosoms would move from left to right, but the bra remained steadfast, pointing straight ahead at your partner. This made it tough for him to decide which set to follow and he often ended up across the room dancing by himself.

Historical Point of Interest: *This bra went out of vogue for a short time in the late 60's when breasts did, too. However, it was brought back into full raging popularity in the 70's when the girls began to notice how flattering it looked on David Bowie.*

THE BULLET BRA: The popular bullet bra of the fifties had cups which were stitched with 500 concentric circles of surgical steel thread, squeezing each breast into a point sharper than a military saber. In order to protect the unsuspecting public, the manufacturer had to sew a warning label into the bra advising just how close you could dance with your date before both his lungs would be irrevocably punctured.

After removing the bra at the end of the night, each breast would still retain it's torpedo-tipped shape for at least 12 hours afterwards. This phe-

SNAGGING YOUR MAN — 50'S STYLE

nomenon was the same as when a baby retained its bullet shaped head for weeks after a low forcep delivery. Thanks to this bra, women have no doubt as to where they came up with the name for the stylish 50's series, "Twin Peaks." Let's face it. Men have always had a thing for breasts. And the ones that were sharp enough to snag a guy's sweater ALWAYS ended up snagging the guy, too.

THE PUSH UP: These bras were constructed in such a way that they could even make Twiggy look like a 36D. Stuffed with padding on the underside of the cups and wired on both sides, they pushed every teeny bit of mammary tissue up and out for maximum viewing pleasure. The only downside was that there was no "thrill of discovery" in the rare event your date managed to unfasten this bra. Instead, he would suffer major disappointment upon finding out that your voluptuous cleavage was a cheap carnival trick of illusion. Sadly, he was left looking at a chest with boobs no bigger than his kid sister's.

THE FRENCH CUT-OUTS: Good old Frederick from—where else but Hollywood—was the first bra maker who made billions by snipping off the ends of the cups. This not only saved money in fabric costs, but Frederick made his first million from the donations of gratitude sent in by men all across America. These dare-to-be-bare styles exposing the nipple were worn by only the trampiest females who knew how to get what they wanted using this "short cut."

Because the 50's nipple was a rare anatomical find, never before seen poking out under clothing, many men didn't know what they were. But one hug

6

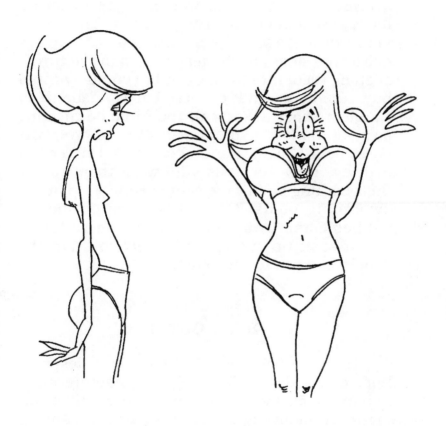

PRESTO! BREASTO!

from a woman wearing this bra, and it didn't take an M.D. to figure out what he was feeling.

FALSIES: Long before breast implants arrived on the scene, women were ordering falsies from their favorite catalogs. They were made of sponge rubber, and women always chose the absolute hugest size manufactured, slipping them into the biggest bra cup they could buy. The sheer bulk of these babies made them excellent shock absorbers. You could be cheering away at Yankee stadium, get hit dead-on in the chest by a Mickey Mantle homer, and never feel a thing. However, gals who wore them under their bathing suits were cautioned to keep out of swimming pools. Once this mass of sponge rubber came into contact with the water, it would soak up enough cubic feet to drain the pool level down to your knees.

BUST OUT!!!

Taking advantage of our teenage desperation, many clever sleezeball manufacturers got rich in the 50's with bogus inventions— all claiming to dramatically increase breast size. Among the more infamous were:

THE BEAUTEOUS-BREAST MACHINE: This was offered in the back of most magazines and claimed to increase your cup size after a month of treatment. All you had to do was place a plastic funnel cup over your breast and hook up the attached hose to the faucet. Then turn it on

TRYING TO MAKE A
MOUNTAIN OUT OF A MOLEHILL

and let 'er rip! The theory behind this was that if you water anything long enough, it will eventually grow. Of course, women watered every night for months in vain. However, the truly determined gals remained undaunted. They simply replaced the water hose with their Hoover hose and successfully raised a few millimeters by the force of pure suction alone.

ISOMETRICS: The daily ritual of almost every girl in the 50's was to clasp her palms together and squeeze while repeating the following:

"I must... I must... I must develop my bust".....

Although it had no real effect, this practice gave rise to the popular cult chanting of the 70's. And instead of raising womens' boobs, it did a lot to raise their consciousness to a state where they no longer gave a damn if they had any at all.

THE MARK EDEN BUST DEVELOPER: Although they were in high demand, it seems nobody can remember what this thing looked like or how it worked. And whether it accomplished what it claimed is still a matter of debate at all National Security Council meetings held after hours. But one thing was for sure, it built up womens' biceps and triceps to a point where we all looked like the American Gladiators. So, no matter what size breast it developed, we now had the added ability to cold-cock any muscle-bound jerk who tried to feel one up on a date.

MORE UNDERCOVER STUFF

THE GIRDLE: The 50's girdle was brought to you by the same people who manufactured steel belted radials in Akron, Ohio. Made from crude neoprene, these garments were built to withstand 15,000 pounds of female cellulite packed under perilous pressure. It was common in the fifties to hear about teenage girls who suffered a spontaneous "blow out" on the dance floor during those dangerous slow dancing dips.

Stretching from waist to mid-thigh, the girdles strained to reduce both of these anatomical areas into roughly the same circumference. Because they had metal garter clasps which dug into the flesh, most women were able to tell their age by counting the rings of broken veins indelibly etched around their thighs.

The good news for parents was that the girdle served another purpose— and that was **birth control.** There wasn't a teenage boy alive in the 50's who had either the strength or patience on a date to successfully peel one of those babies off his babe. And even if by some miracle he succeeded, the sight of the mushrooming cellulite released from the flab under pressure would've stopped even the horniest guy dead in his tracks.

Historical Point of Interest: *One teenage guy who witnessed this ghastly sight in the front seat of his Dodge cleverly used this haunting memory to invent the first safety air bag installed in today's automobiles.*

THE FIFTIES GIRDLE:
CAUTION – CONTENTS UNDER PRESSURE

The gals of the 50's went through an awful lot of time and trouble to show-off parts of their anatomy that no guy was allowed to lay a hand on. Breasts were there to "tease" not to "please." In the 50's, sexual expression was taboo and sexual frustration was rampant. Most teens were so horny all the time, it's no wonder the gals were covered with zits and the guys were nearly blind from doing what their parents kept warning them not to do.

QUIZ 1

1. Scarlett O'Hara's Merry Widow bra was manufactured during the Civil War by:

>a. Dixie Cups
>
>b. Jimmy Carter & Co.
>
>c. Rhett's butler
>
>d. Rhett's butt
>
>** a. it later merged with b to become Dixie Carter.*

2. Before the silicone breast implant, many Hollywood stars had which surgery performed to make their breasts look bigger:

>a. rib removal
>
>b. beach ball implants
>
>c. implanting 3-D lenses in their eyes
>
>d. lobotomy
>
>** d. the operation just made them THINK they were bigger.*

3. What protection did Jayne Mansfield have to insure the safety of her famous breasts?

>a. $1,000,000 policy from Lloyds of London
>
>b. tupperware bra cups
>
>c. she packed a Colt 45 in each bra cup
>
>d. Mickey Hargitay's 20 inch biceps
>
>** c. plus there was room left over for a Howitzer.*

4. The way to attract the most attention with the French Cut-Out bra was to wear it:

> a. under a skin-tight sweater

> b. while cheerleading

> c. while nursing in public

> d. in a cold room

> ** d. below 32 degrees F.*

5. What was the only 100% effective birth control method in the fifties?

> a. abstention

> b. the formica diaphragm

> c. wearing a girdle to bed

> d. not wearing a girdle to bed

> ** both c and d were pretty unappetizing.*

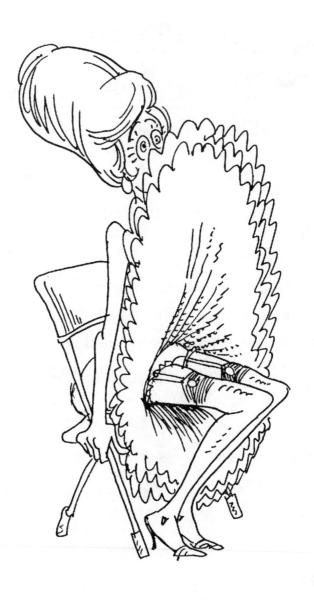

TONIGHT, WE HAVE
A REALLY BIG SHOW

CHAPTER 2

FIFTIES PROM PROTOCOL: FOSSILIZED IN STONE

THE 50's PROM GOWN

It had to be powder-puff pink, it had to be strapless, and it had to have a brutally stiff net stole to qualify as a bona fide 1950's Prom Gown. And the stays in the gown plus the Merry Widow made it just about impossible to breathe. So we would prop ourselves up by hanging both arms around our date's neck while he pushed our limp dishrag bodies around the dance floor all night. This did wonders for our date's ego. Even if you would have preferred going to the prom with an inbred cousin, when you danced with a guy this way, he automatically assumed you were so crazy about him that you just couldn't keep your hands off him.

GETTING STIFF: NO ALCOHOL REQUIRED

The Cardinal Rule of Prom Gowns was that they had to be worn with no less than six freshly starched crinolines underneath. In the starching process, the following steps were ALWAYS taken to insure the crinoline stood out at a 90 degree angle from your body:

1. They were soaked for a full week in a super-saturated solution of sugar and water.

2. Next they were dried over an opened umbrella for a week.

3. Finally, they were sprayed with enough starch to feed the country of Italy for a year.

The resulting product was about as flexible as Don King's hair. In fact, if you tried to sit down in the crinolines, the front of your gown usually flew up over your face. And naturally, there were those guys who were just so "polite" that they'd be getting a chair for you every two seconds— then running around the front to reap the benefits of the floor show.

STAND BY YOUR MAN

Because it was impossible to sit down, we were forced to spend the evening wandering around the gym in our four-inch excruciatingly painful stiletto heels gulping down Triple Strength Bufferins with our punch. And speaking of punch, a gal didn't dare bend over the refreshment table to pour herself a cup for fear that the wads of Kleenex stuffed in her cups might spill out into the bowl.

And do you remember how those starched crinolines shredded our good nylon stockings so it looked like we were wearing old woolen sweaters on our legs? But the absolute worst was the way the ten rows of stiff ruffled netting on the bodice chafed our underarms until they looked like we had a terminal case of razor burn.

DYED-TO-MATCH SHOES

Naturally, no prom night was complete without the obligatory torrential downpour. This spelled ruination for two things—the first being your satin shoes. You know, the pair that the shoe salesman spent three weeks dyeing in the Ted Turner Colorizing Studio located in the back room of the store. The poor man experienced more than his share of Maalox Moments trying to get an exact match with the dirty fabric swatch we carried around in our purses for months beforehand. And we never gave him a moment's peace until he got a color match so close it was within a UV light band either way.

Historical Point of Interest: *the process they eventually developed to get an exact match became so technically sophisticated, it was duplicated by the A.M.A. and is currently used in hospitals all over the country to find organ donors.*

We were just lucky that the salesman didn't accompany us to the prom. Because after traipsing through several puddles to get to the car, the shoe dye ran all over the floor mats of our boyfriend's '55 Chevy. And nobody enjoys making out while a shoe salesman is sobbing loudly in the back seat.

REACHING NEW HEIGHTS: THE BEEHIVE

The second catastrophe produced by the rain was the sudden collapse of our beehive hairdos. If you remember, this hairstyle was an architectural feat equal to the Great Pyramid at Cheops. And the beehive was nearly as tall, too. How tall was it? Well, you could sell lift tickets for one of these things.

To whip one of these do's into shape required a solid hour-and-a-half of teasing the hair until every single shaft was split up into 10,000 micro-hairs. This produced the desired effect of increasing its total volume to about twenty-five cubic feet. We're talking about hair that looked like a barrel of Jiffy Pop just before it's ready to blow.

CAUTION: THE BEEHIVE CAN BE HAZARDOUS TO YOUR HEALTH

It usually took about three hairdressers to complete a beehive. This was because the first two dropped to the floor after the ten cans of hair spray they were inhaling lacquered their bronchial tubes shut. But once you got past the third operator, you had it made. Finally, the top layer of teased hair was smoothed and coaxed around a pre-fab styrofoam cone, duplicating the shape of the bee-hive to perfection. Luckily, in the 50's, we never had to worry about having a "bad hair day." When we wore one of these coiffures, we looked bad EVERYDAY.

No self-respecting gal of the 50's would take the fashion risk of forgetting to add the "Fuzzy Bee" hair ornament for the crowning touch. Mounted on steel picks which strategically pierced the hive at five different levels, it took the steady hand of a seasoned pro to execute this to exact perfection. One false move, and an area of vital brain function could be destroyed—like the frog you pithed that afternoon in Biology Lab.

The finishing touch was accomplished with a can of spray-on glitter—de rigueur for that totally "devastating" look. A glittering head insured true "Prom Magic." But after running through the parking lot in gusts of sheeting rain to reach the gym, there was hardly anything magical about a beehive that had collapsed into a pancake with the glitter cascading into your cleavage.

PETALS FROM HEAVEN:
THE WRIST CORSAGE

The wrist corsage was the ONLY way to go in those days. And we insisted that ours be made from gardenias. However, since this variety could not survive a climate north of El Paso, they became brown and withered by the time we hit the dance floor. Frequently, they died several hours before your date arrived, forcing him to present them to you in a *pine box.* And when we arrived at the dance and our dates slipped off our little fake fur bunny jackets, the petals were stripped off and fell around our feet, sticking to our wet shoes. In many cases, this was an omen that more than one thing might be de-flowered before the night was over.

PROMS OF THE 90's

Today's proms retain very little of the old 50's charm. They have evolved and mutated into larger-than-life extravaganzas reaching the epic proportions of a Spielberg production. And they cost about the same, too. Today's parents have been known to refinance their homes to pay for the gowns, tuxes, tickets, dinners, limos, and after-prom parties—which are all a necessary part of this rite of passage. Here's an encapsulated account of the new twists on old traditions in the proms of the 90's...

THE LIMO: SEX ED ON WHEELS

Any teenage guy today who considers himself "cool" would never be caught dead driving to the prom in his parent's pathetic Ford Escort. It would take a full-time P.R. agency two years to reverse the damage inflicted upon the guy's image. The limo at $75.00 an hour with a well-stocked bar is the only way to go. Equipped with a chauffeur placed under a gag order and featuring soundproof, smoked-plate glass dividing the front and back seats, these vehicles offer the ultimate in discretion for their perpetually horny high school passengers.

Naturally, the limo companies go to great lengths to get the competitive edge. And the truly enterprising ones feature the steamy Kevin Costner/Sean Young scene from "No Way Out" on a continuous reel from their built-in VCR's. In case you happen to be the one person left on earth who isn't familiar with this classic scene, it features the most educational and erotic love scene of **Inventive Limo Foreplay** ever put on celluloid. And, of course, the kids give it their best shot trying to reproduce these scenes live in the back seat. This insures the crafty limo companies that there will be at least four extra hours of driving time while the kids are busy proving that practice makes perfect.

THE PROM GOWN:
A REAL STRETCH FROM THE 50's

One word says it all: S-P-A-N-D-E-X. All that tight-fitting rubber we used to wear under our prom gowns ARE the prom gowns now. And it's stretched to the limit over well-defined muscle that has been pumped up with diligent daily Nautilus workouts. We're talking unibody outfits here— no seams— no hooks— no buttons— no darts. It's "One Size (Attempts To) Fit All" couture in colors from day-glo orange to electric blue.

Luckily for the guys, these human inner tubes have provided built-in easy access by the ingenious modern day invention of velcro. So it's possible for a fellow to have both hands on his Kevin Costner Manual and rip open a velcro tab with his teeth at the same time. To maintain the total sleekness of this look, it goes without saying that wearing any kind of bra with this outfit is completely outlawed. In fact, the only piece of underwear under spandex approved by the High School Fashion Board for Babes is a microscopic butt-string bikini.

"I DIDN'T SEE ANYTHING.
DID YOU SEE ANYTHING?"
"NOPE, I DIDN'T SEE ANYTHING."

DIRTY DANCING: DIP AND WHIP

The kids immediately flock to the dance floor to do the Lambada, executing some moves that are so bold they would have given Arthur Murray a major coronary. The girls never have to worry about falling out of their dresses because they ARE out of them already when this dance heats up the floor. Most of the chaperons would rather stand blindfolded on the sidelines than be named as accomplices to what is taking place before their eyes.

The traditional "Goodnight Sweetheart" dance played at midnight has been replaced by 2 Live Crew's more promising "Me So Horny." This song is performed live by a rap group who is so raunchy, their only ambition is to get through at least half of the song before being hauled off to the slammer.

AFTER PROM PARTIES: BOOK ME DANNO

Kids in the 90's don't stand on ceremony when it comes to past prom traditions. They're out there making new ones like booking their after-prom parties in hotel rooms. Though their parents are hor- rified, the local merchants are jumping for joy. Prom time translates into mega-bucks for everybody.

1. The video stores are only too happy to supply the hotels with a variety of Showtime "After Hours" flicks ranging from the Prom Night Slasher genre to the latest religious releases. The most popular are from authorities like Jimmy Swaggart—who offers a divinely instructional

WE DELIVER!
IN AND OUT IN NO TIME

video on how to get the best religious experience in a hotel room during a five minute period. It's offered compliments of the hotel and placed at no extra charge next to the Gideon Bibles.

2. The pharmaceutical companies love to send out their crack team of all-night detail men. They go room to room, dispensing graduation favors from their briefcases filled with their specialty product, *"Cap N' Gown Condoms."* This is one place where a "raincoat" would certainly do nothing to dampen the evening's festivities.

3. And the local breweries have the solution to a life and death situation for prom kids: the keg running dry. They dispatch trained St. Bernards with coin-op barrels of brewskis tied around their necks.

It's safe to say that the Prom Night has always been a serious concern for parents everywhere. The event really hasn't changed all that much in forty years; it's actually come full circle:

THEN: the gals used to come home from the dance with frizzy hair, torn crinolines, and smudged eye makeup.

NOW: they leave for the prom looking this way.

Bullet bras and crinolines haven't left the scene of the prom either after all these years. Now they're *making* scenes at the prom. Compared with all the fuss of shoe-matching, gown-starching, and all the other things that took so much of our time, today's formal wear is quite maintenance free. Now the only thing girls have to do after an active prom night is take their steel radial bustiers in to be rotated.

QUIZ 2

1. A guy's most thrilling prom moment was when he saw you:

    a. gracefully waltz down the stairs at your home

    b. close your eyes to kiss him

    c. putting on the corsage he bought for you

    d. taking off your Merry Widow bra

    d. hopefully, you removed the Kleenex first.

2. On the night of the prom, girls were warned by their Moms' not to lose:

    a. the pearl earrings they lent you

    b. one of their long white gloves

    c. their Dad's expensive camera

    d. their virginity

    d. that was one thing that couldn't be replaced.

3. What ritual is performed by all fathers for their daughters on the night of the prom?:

    a. having the first dance with her at home

    b. taking thousands of photos of her before she leaves

    c. giving her date the old "responsibility" lecture

d. locking her chastity belt

d. and throwing away the key until her wedding night.

4. Prom photos were taken by professionals and later used:

    a. in the high school yearbook

    b. to send to all your relatives

    c. to make a treasured scrapbook

    d. for blackmail

    d. the entire senior class collectively owed $5 million.

5. The average teenage girl spent a great deal of pre-prom time getting fitted:

    a. with a specially made Merry Widow bra

    b. with a tailor-made strapless gown

    c. with an elaborate hairpiece

    d. with a diaphragm

    d. the Ob-gyns offered prom discounts.

THE FIFTIES GOOD GIRL:
LOOK, BUT DON'T TOUCH

CHAPTER 3

SEX IN THE FIFTIES:
THE GREAT DEPRESSION

50's MOTTO:
IF IT FEELS GOOD, REPRESS IT

There was no guesswork to dating in the 50's. We followed the same rules that were put forth in Biblical times. The "Ten Commandments of Dating" were carved on two Baby Ruth bars and brought down from Mount Acne by Sandra Dee and Tab Hunter. The commandments all started out with "Thou Shalt Not..." and banned everything that was fun. Also, if you donned the appropriate pair of red and green glasses, you could read them in 3-D.

First of all, they divided all of Pubescent Sexdom into two categories—there was no in-between. You were either:

1. A **GOOD** girl or a **GOOD** boy

2. Or a **BAD** girl or a **BAD** boy

Good girls were named Kathy or Peggy. Bad girls were named DeeDee or Angie. All boys named Johnny were bad. We learned this from watching classic teenage sagas like "A Summer Place" and "Where The Boys Are." Everything your parents never told you about sex was contained in these films.

31

THE DOUBLE STANDARD:
DATING FOR THE GOOD AND THE BAD

GOOD GIRLS: followed this strict protocol on a date:

The local movie theater— middle row. No hands allowed dangling below the shoulders.

BAD GIRLS: did a variation on the same theme:

Drive-in theater— last row— back seat. Hands, arms, or legs often dangling out of car windows.

GOOD GIRLS: Immediately after the movie you went straight to Ho-Jo's for a hot dog and an ice cream soda.

BAD GIRLS: Six-pack from the snack bar obtained using false I.D.— warmed by interior car temperature to approximately 113 degrees.

GOOD GIRLS: The boy must go all the way to the front door with you.

BAD GIRLS: The boy must go all the way WITH you before you get to the front door.

GOOD GIRLS: One goodnight kiss allowed on the front porch before your Dad slips his hand through the doorway and yanks you inside by the scruff of your neck.

BAD GIRLS: Make out until dawn in the empty parking lot behind the supermarket. Sneak in through the back door where you run into your Dad who is doing the same thing after a late night at the

local bar.

GOOD GIRLS: Small amount of lipstick on his collar permissible.

BAD GIRLS: Lots of lipstick on his shorts mandatory.

GOOD GIRLS: Act put out if a guy tries to make a pass.

BAD GIRLS: Put out.

50's GREASERS: THE STRAIGHT MEN

There was no doubt about the gender identification of a 50's guy. Men were not into the "sensitivity" thing like they are today. You know— the kind of guy who orders a Perrier and motivational tape at a bar, then holds your hair back while you throw up.

Our guys back in the 50's knew how to act like REAL men. They wore greased-down duck tails, black leather jackets, and carried a CARTON of cigarettes rolled up in their T-shirt sleeves. They rode Harleys and went to biker bars where Jack Daniels was served *on tap.* Light beer and light loafers were never found in a 50's bar. Our guys were the kind that cruised into a bar and ordered a beer and a bowl of nails to snack on. And low alcohol beer was only for geeks who didn't want to get drunk, but liked to urinate.

A DUCKTAIL, PEGGED PANTS AND
A PACK OF WEEDS...
IT DOESN'T GET ANY COOLER THAN THIS.

REAL MEN: BAD SEX

However, bad boys of the 50's were all talk and little action when it came to the sex department. Even though all the Johnnys carried "safes" around in their wallets, they remained there unused for so long that they formed a permanent ring embossed in the leather. In fact, if they tried to pry it off, it disintegrated from age.

Girls found out the hard way that the Johnnys who referred to themselves as "Magnificent Stallions" often ended up beating a *dead horse.* The only time things got hot in their bedrooms was when the air conditioner broke down. Premarital sex was labeled a sin back then, and the way those guys did it was really a crime! It wasn't Johnny's fault though. What kind of sexual technique could a guy learn from Tab Hunter movies? It would be like taking birth control advice from Ethyl Kennedy.

50's PERFORMANCE:
THE UNDERACHIEVERS

Having your first sexual experience with one of these greasers was, to put it bluntly, anti-climatic. The kind of guy who boasted that he made love "like an animal", was in truth, taking a *step up* from his place on the evolutionary ladder. And when he bragged about being able to make love non-stop for an hour and five minutes, you could be sure it was on the night we set the clocks ahead. With the kind of "staying power" these guys had, they should have stayed home. They were not the swiftest sweet-talkers in the sack, either. About the only time they talked to us was when they told us to "wake up."

But most of us really didn't mind back then. Because the majority of girls in the 50's usually stopped just short of "going all the way." Just at the point of no return, Donna Reed would come in and take over our bodies. However, we did engage in more heavy petting than you'd find at most zoos. Compared to the sexual activity that goes on today though, we were merely goody two-shoes with our knees welded together.

Sex in the 90's is a whole different ball game. There are no longer "good" and "bad" categories of teenagers. The old commandments spelled out in black and white have been replaced by technicolor guidelines that allow sex to become a "personal" decision. Translated, this means for everyone else to butt out.

Let's take a look at some of the contributing factors to the sexual promiscuity so prevalent in the 90's.

TEENAGE MOVIES:
HEATING UP THE SEATS

Just watching a typical brat pack movie depicting teenage sexual activities in the 90's is enough to make you head for the nearest cold shower. There's no such thing as an "innocent" first kiss anymore. Today's kids kiss like *Pez dispensers:* their heads fold back 180 degrees and their tongues pop out.

PANT–PANT

And the kids watching these films are becoming sexually active at younger and younger ages. At this rate, they'll soon be packing condoms in Bazooka bubble gum. The shocking thing is how girls are being portrayed in these teenage flicks as totally sexually promiscuous with no conscience. Every five minutes, there is another gratuitous sex scene showing the same girl making love with a different guy. Today's girls go through guys so fast, they need speed bumps installed outside their bedroom doors.

The teenage stars of today are so addicted to sex, most of them donate their free time making training films for Dr. Ruth. Another sad thing is that the girls in today's films have lost that healthy, wholesome look. Their decadent lifestyles have made them ill. A case in point is the girl who starred in "Debbie Does Dallas." The poor thing was **bedridden** for more than half the movie.

CONDOM COMPANIES:
STRONG BUT SENSITIVE

Having "safe sex" in the 50's meant your parents didn't find out. Today, it's having an air bag installed on your headboard.

And now there's a whole raft of sexually transmitted diseases we should all be worrying about. Sex in the 90's is dangerous: so if you're going to party, you've got to WEAR YOUR PARTY HAT. It's either that or boil your date before you sleep together.

It should come as no big shock that the personal products companies are having record sales. Drug stores have added extra shelves with displays of condoms to meet your every need. You can even buy ribbed condoms for barbecues and glow-in-the-dark neon condoms for the visually impaired.

We've come a long way from the pimply-faced kid of the 50's who circled the counter like a nervous pup, trying to get up the courage to ask the druggist for a pack of Trojans. Now they're being hawked over the loud speakers in all the chain stores, often as the "Blue Light Special." It won't be long before we see the inevitable ad on TV featuring the "Dancing Condoms" singing "What I Did For Love."

Everybody is getting into the act to make a buck. These embarrassing products have now replaced the traditional homemaker's tupperware parties. But the sales pitch hasn't changed; they still boast a *perfect seal* and *watertight fit.*

TELEPHONE SEX LINES: 1-900-SICKKOO

Fearing it might be left out of the sexual market boom, even Ma Bell has gotten into the act by adopting a new slogan for the 90's— "Reach Out and Touch THIS!" The new phenomenon of "party lines" that cater to a bunch of sex-starved maggots talking dirty to each other for hours is making the phone companies even richer.

Every sicko in the country is getting his jollies

without leaving the phone; much less home. So as not to be discriminatory in their business practice, the phone companies now offer phone sex with **call waiting** for masochists.

The main attraction in phone sex is that it's a relatively safe way to get off without getting a disease. Other than possibly contracting an occasional ear infection, this method gives the safest sex of all.

ADVICE TO THE SEXUALLY STALEMATED

Today's relationships differ from those of our parents' generation mostly in the lack of commitment. In the 50's, you went steady with the same guy for four years in high school and ended up marrying him. Nowadays, after dating the same guy for four weeks, he'll usually tell you that he wants to see other people.

So tell him to go watch **Donahue.**

Another common complaint often voiced by a young, single man is that he doesn't like to use condoms. He'll bitch and moan that when he wears one, "I can't feel anything."

So tell him that makes **two** of you.

Men say they can't commit because Women's Lib made women too demanding. The females have become so aggressive in the lovemaking department, it's scaring the males to death. And maybe they have a point. For instance, the old lovemaking scenario

41

went like this:

Kiss...kiss... touch...touch... groan...groan... and it was over.

Now the guys need a Geography degree to locate your G Spot. They need to master 123 positions from the Kama Sutra, and have to leave the room in shame if they reach orgasm two seconds before you do. Because of this, the most common sexual dysfunction in today's society is ***"premature evacuation."*** It seems the old, positive approaches like "I'm O.K., You're O.K." are being replaced by the 90's philosophy— "I'm Dysfunctional, You're Hopeless"— but that's okay too.

The point is that in the 90's, we still feel the same guilts, fears, and uncertainties as we did in the 50's. But now, hey— it's hip to feel good about feeling lousy.

QUIZ 3

1. Connie Stevens and Tab Hunter never had sex in all those teenage movies because he:

   a. kept forgetting where he put his condoms

   b. kept forgetting where to put it on

   c. couldn't get up the nerve

   d. couldn't get it up

   * *b and also where to put it in.*

2. The movies of the fifties always had a moral. After the bad girl succumbed to sex in "Where The Boys Are" she:

   a. got hit by a car

   b. got pregnant

   c. was sorry she didn't try it sooner

   d. got more dates than ever

   * *d. And lived happily ever after, too.*

3. "Heavy petting" in the 50's was defined as "Any physical contact...."

   a. occurring below the waist

   b. accompanied by sexual arousal

   c. with an animal

   d. that put a smile on your face

   * *c and d, especially if he was on the football team.*

4. The movie "Basic Instinct" showed us that fear heightens sexual arousal. What did the audience fear most?

> a. the ice pick
>
> b. Michael Douglas's bare butt cheeks
>
> c. that Sharon would put her underpants on
>
> d. that Sharon would forget how to cross her legs
>
> ** b. if you sat in the front row, it was sheer terror.*

5. A "sensitive" way of letting your guy know that his difficulty in staying sexually aroused is bothering you is to:

> a. hand him a ruler and some tape
>
> b. put it in a permanent cast
>
> c. give him a can of spray starch
>
> d. use a stopwatch and clock his usual 15 seconds
>
> ** d. then start climbing the walls for added emphasis.*

CHAPTER 4

FIFTIES CONFESSION:
PAROLE FOR THE SOUL

CONFESSION: PRAY FOR YOUR THRILLS

It was tough enough growing up in the 50's, but growing up Catholic was murder. Catholicism is a religion based on guilt, a lot like the Jewish faith, except with different holidays. This is one church that has more rules than an Olympic committee. But they worked. You were indoctrinated to be so scared of committing a MORTAL SIN (as opposed to a venial sin) and having to confess it, that it always kept you on the straight and narrow. Almost anything a teenager did was classified as a *venial sin,* and if it FELT GOOD, it was a *mortal sin.* And if it FELT REALLY GREAT, it was a *multiple transgression.*

AUTOBIOGRAPHY:
PORTRAIT OF A TEENAGE SINNER

The following is a true anecdote from my days as a teenager and is typical of almost every other Catholic girl's experience in that era. It also illustrates why fear and guilt were a way of life in the 50's, as I stated in the introduction. Also, it is my unselfish hope that sharing my tawdry experience will be of great psychological help to all women —

45

and possibly land me a guest spot on Sally Jesse Raphael.

THE TAWDRY TALE: HERE GOES........

In our parish, two priests heard confessions on a regular basis. The one who sat in the confessional booth on the left side of the church was Father Merciful. All the kids rushed to his side, because he didn't ask too many embarrassing questions and gave out mild penances. However, on the other side sat the infamous Father Purgatorio who was as ruthless in cross examination as Perry Mason, as relentless in handing out penances as Torquemada, and as DEAF as a stone. One consequence of his deafness was that he would repeat your sins so loudly, it would have been far less public to confess them on Oprah.

THE SATURDAY MORNING:
AFTER THE FRIDAY NIGHT BEFORE

Needless to say, on Saturday afternoons the two confessional lines were hardly equal in length. Merciful's line was as long as what you'd expect for a James Dean film, while Purgatorio's was the same as you'd see for a re-run of Ishtar. And when we arrived freshly tarnished from our Friday night dates, my girlfriends and I always stood in Merciful's line. But this was often our undoing, because Purgatorio would regularly emerge from his confessional and order half of Merciful's line over to his side. When

47

this happened, it was like crossing over the Berlin Wall, which was still standing in those days (next to Purgatorio, in fact).

So there we stood, wringing our hands and trembling with indecision. We did not want to be subjected to the public broadcast of our sins by Purgatorio, but we couldn't ditch our confessional duties either. We were clearly sitting on a dilemma with horns bigger than Warren Beatty's on a Saturday night.

So we devised THE PLAN: We went home and returned *incognito* wearing trench coats, shades, and chiffon scarves wrapped around our heads. If we were going to have our most intimate transgressions broadcast, hopefully no one we knew would be able to finger us. It is painfully apparent at this point in the story, that your average Muslim woman had more street smarts than we did.

THE CROSS-EXAMINATION: BEING NAILED TO THE CROSS

After we went back into the church in disguise and got in line, predictably, Purgatorio stuck his head out of his confessional and barked:

"Come on—come over here. You with the scarf—you're next," pointing a finger longer and bonier than Arsenio's at me.

Suddenly I was filled with a divine revelation about the priesthood: Celibacy can sure make you nasty.

So I made my way on wobbly legs into the booth. He tore back the confessional screen so fast, a sonic boom rattled the windows.

"Go ahead," he said gruffly.

"Bless me Father, for I have sinned. It has been two weeks since my last confession."

To which the congregation heard only his resounding voice yell out:

"HOW MANY?"

Uh..two weeks and..er...um..I used the Lord's name in vain Father."

"You did WHAT?" he yelled.

"I sw..sw..swore, Father...and er..uh... I had *lewd* thoughts, too."

"You got SCREWED?" he screamed incedulously.

"No...No... I had lewd *thoughts*," I croaked. I was close to wetting my pants now.

"How MANY TIMES?" he roared.

" Twice. And I also sneaked out on a date against my parents' wishes."

"You did IT with a BOY?"

"Uh...yes...but I felt guilty and came right home again," I whimpered.

TEN HAIL MARYS WASN'T ENOUGH

"How LONG did it take you TO DO THAT?" he boomed out.

"Uh..only a few minutes. It was raining and I got so soaked, we came right home," I tried to explain.

"And you didn't bring RUBBERS?" he charged.

"No....but I won't do it again, Father." I felt like dying at this point.

"That was irresponsible. DON'T EVER DO IT AGAIN!" he barked loudly.

"I won't, I promise."

"Now BE A GOOD GIRL and say 10 Hail Mary's...you'd better make that 100 Hail Marys...and mind your parents. Go in peace and God bless you."

PENANCE:
TEN MINUTES OF PUBLIC HUMILIATION
AND TEN HAIL MARYS LATER

I emerged, crawling lower than a worm all the way down the aisle toward the altar. I looked guiltier than one of the defendants on "The People's Court" and figured everyone in the place must think I had tried more men than Judge Wapner. My girlfriends headed straight for the nearest exit. In fact, there wasn't a soul past puberty left standing in line.

I said my penance and walked backwards all the way down the aisle towards Freedom. Scenes from the "Longest Mile" kept replaying in my sinner's head.

The whole gang was standing there waiting for me absolutely dumbstruck. I looked down at my chest to see if a Scarlet A had materialized there.

"Wow! You actually did **it**. You really did **it**!" they said with a new tone of reverence in their voices. "We want all the details— and don't leave ANYTHING out!" they begged.

I thought about pleading my case but knew it would be entirely futile. A bunch of 16-year-old girls with pubescent hormones raging through their bodies know no other interpretation than the sexual one. So I cocked my elbow and strutted down the steps. Far be it from me to besmirch the image of their new heroine.

* * *

Back in those teenage days, we weighed every move we made against what kind of sin it produced. We used to sit and ponder earth shattering questions like— if a French kiss is a mortal sin, is a hickey only a venial? Or— if he accidentally brushes my breast with his arm, do I have to confess it? One thing was for sure. If all of us Catholic girls spent as much time doing our homework as we did trying to find loopholes in our religious doctrine, we would all have been Phi Beta Kappas.

QUIZ 4

1. Many Catholic girls believed that an orgasm was:

   a. contagious

   b. found only in the choir loft

   c. a one-celled microbe

   d. something only Protestant girls had

   * *d. accounted for 100,000 conversions per year.*

2. Catholic girls who French kissed guys:

   a. were doomed to Hell

   b. had an appointed daily confessional time

   c. were regularly "stoned"

   d. were the most popular girls in the class

   * *d. they also spoke in "tongues."*

3. Racy Catholic girls wore their parochial school uniforms:

   a. with knee socks and garter belts

   b. to happy hour

   c. with push-up bras

   d. with diaphragms

   * *d. like the Girl Scouts, they were always prepared.*

4. If a Catholic girl prayed for more than 15 minutes at the altar, you knew she:

   a. was a devout parishioner

   b. was lighting candles for the poor

   c. had a special prayer for world peace

   d. had done the "dirty deed" the night before

   * *d. that and the huge smile on her face was a dead giveaway.*

5. Catholic couples who faithfully practiced the rhythm method probably had:

   a. a deep respect for church policy

   b. sex once a month

   c. eight or more kids

   d. horns about six inches long

   * *all of the above plus about 200 cold showers a month.*

CHAPTER 5

FIFTIES MAKE-UP: BEAUTY SIX FEET DEEP

COSMETIC OVERKILL

During the decades of the fifties and sixties, there were no such things as "state of the art" cosmetics. Department stores did not offer computerized color charts programmed by sexually unidentifiable make-up consultants— dressed in white lab coats wearing spiky hair and six pearlescent shades of eyeshadow. Also, there were no aestheticians lying in wait at every counter trying to suck your pores out. And nobody had a complete mental breakdown trying to choose the correct shade from several hundred samples being applied to your face by desperate salespersons on commission.

SMEAR TACTICS OF THE 50's: PANCAKE MAKE-UP

Back in the 50's life was much simpler, cosmetically speaking. We had only one choice, pancake make-up, which came in two shades— **Mime White** or **Hepatitis Orange.** This stuff had the same consistency as Play-Dough, and when applied properly with a dampened O-Cello sponge, it dried on your face like wet cement. It was so thick, it had the

SIX INCHES THICK...
ONE MORE TO GO

ability to hide the absolute worst cases of teenage acne. Of course, it also eradicated most facial expression lines in the process. This make-up was so thick, we had to use a dip stick to measure each successive application.

THE GREAT TEENAGE TRAGEDY: LOSING FACE

Because of it's waxy consistency, pancake make-up had a low melting point, and one had to avoid the heat at all costs. If you were making out with a guy on the beach under the blazing sun, it was a sure thing that your entire face would melt and slide down into your bra top, lips and all. To the rest of the beach goers it looked like you had just been shot in the chest. But under normal weather conditions, one application of pancake make-up stayed on the face for at least a month.

If you wanted to remove it at night, you would need thousands of cotton balls thoroughly saturated with Janitor-In-A-Drum. And God forbid, if you were lazy and flopped into bed with it still on, even Drano couldn't unclog your pores the next morning.

CAKE MASCARA: A SPIT IN TIME

After the three hours it took the pancake to set up, it was time to apply your cake mascara. This cosmetic staple was packaged in a cute little red plastic box that had a sliding drawer containing a

WHY CAN'T SOMEBODY
INVENT A WATERPROOF MASCARA?

teeny, tiny toothbrush applicator. After daintily removing the brush, we would do the unlady-like thing—yes, we all did it— we'd SPIT into the mascara to soften it up with the brush until it reached about the same consistency as your average dog turd.

Next, we would skillfully apply 10 to 20 coats until our lashes literally drooped with goop—or until we ran out of spit—which was usually the case. Cake mascara was available in one shade only, jet black. And because Jacques Costeau didn't want to get into the business, it wasn't waterproof either. Therefore, crying at the movies or any other public place was taboo. But after a showing of a tear-jerker like "Splendor In The Grass," the dam inevitably broke and we emerged from the theater with those hideous "racoon-eyes."

THE EYELASH CURLER: GRIP AND FLIP

Who could ever forget this handy little gadget? It looked like a pair of miniature forceps with a strip of cushioning rubber that ran along the base. Actually, it kind of worked like forceps too. You had to slip it over your upper lash and once in place, bear down on the spring action with about 400 pounds of pressure per square inch until your lash finally pointed straight up at the ceiling. You remember the look: a pinwheel kind of a thing going on in the eyeballs. We were all trying to achieve the DOE-EYED look of Audrey Hepburn, but what we usually got was the BUG-EYED look of Marty Feldman.

OCULAR SEX: GIVING SAFE EYELASH

In order to prevent eyelash breakage when using the eyelash curler, a little vaseline applied to the tips did wonders. And for those who were heavily into "butterfly kissing" with the eyelashes (considered merely a venial sin in the 50's), KY Jelly was a smart substitute.

And how many times did our mothers' warn us never to use our eyelash curlers when we were in a hurry? We were all subjected to the horror stories about how Aunt Margaret's slip of the hand rendered her eyelids permanently rolled back so she was never again able to sleep with her eyes closed. But we didn't care about stuff like that. If that's what it took to have that Sandra Dee "innocent wide-eyed" look, we felt it was worth sleeping with blinders on for the rest of our lives.

THE BIG KISS-OFF: TANGEE LIPSTICK

This was THE favorite Five and Dime Store standard of the fifties. No matter what shade you bought, from the popular **Wild Fuschia** to **Drop Dead White**, it ALWAYS turned *orange* on the lips. And once it was applied, it was an absolute must to blot for several hundred successive smacks with those little tissue blotting papers. Why? Nobody knew why. But nobody had the guts to find out what would happen if you didn't.

Historical Point of Interest: *after teenage girls abandoned the blotting practice, this diminutive tissue made a huge comeback in the 70's as roll-your-own joint papers.*

This brand's claim to fame was in calling it the first "smear-proof" lipstick. And hundreds of teenage girls who had just come into their first "heat" put this claim to the test in rigorous week long make-out sessions with their boyfriends. During these ultra-passionate sessions, the gals often suffered vicious beard burns and teeth ground down to the dentin. But happily, the claims were true and the lipstick remained steadfast on their lips as well as on their boyfriends' shorts.

HELEN NEUSCHAFER NAIL GLITZ: BREATHTAKING!

Helen was the innovator who first suspended 500,000 pulverized pieces of multicolored glitter in clear polish, creating the world's first nail glitz. She stumbled onto the idea (literally) when she tripped and fell into her kid's sand-box with wet nails.

No well-groomed gal of the day would be caught dead without this Woolworth's best seller on her nails. The main reason for the popularity of Helen's nail polish was because it was cheaper than any other polish on the market— including furniture. We were totally enthralled, as we faithfully painted this clumpy mess on our finger and toe nails every Friday night spanning the decade. There was only one drawback — the stuff NEVER really dried. Most of us when the product was hyped as "so spectacular, it'll leave you breathless."

STEEL CURLERS: MAKING A BIG IMPRESSION

Remember those huge steel bouffant rollers we set our hair with every night? One restless night's sleep on these babies could inflict a brain contusion that left you unable to read anything but Dick and Jane Primers for the rest of your natural life. For the best results, you would roll up and sit for at least three hours under the hair dryer with the ridiculous looking plastic bouffant hood that had one heat setting— FRY. If the dryer could make it through the first hour without sustaining a nuclear meltdown, you emerged coiffed for life.

However, due to the high heat conductivity of the metal rollers, most teenage girls emerged with an unpleasant side effect: third degree roller burns over 90% of their scalps. This not only left you with permanent ridges in your hair but, unfortunately, in your skull bones too.

Historical Point of Interest: *In the late 60's this look caught the attention of Hollywood's keen eye and served as the inspiration for the **Klingon Heads** of Star Trek.*

COSMETICS TODAY:
A MOLECULAR CRAPSHOOT

Today, the purchase of cosmetics is dictated by what is considered **politically** and **ecologically** correct. No gal in her right mind wants to risk getting neutered by a rabid SPCA activist because her make-up was tested on helpless **killer rats** in some lab outside of Rahway, New Jersey.

Not only that, but it takes a Ph.D in chemistry to understand what the products are made of nowadays. They now list ingredients on make-up labels like "hydrating molecular compounds," "alpha-hydoxy acid," "placental compounds," and "retinoic acid." And there are countless articles hyping the anti-aging products, explaining how they interfere with free radicals. Wasn't it a lot easier back in the 60's when a free radical was just a doped-up hippie?

Now we're using molecular hairsetters, microchip suspended mascara, and silicate light-diffusing base make-ups. The choices alone are enough to give you a mega-ton headache.

QUIZ 5

1. In the 50's, hair conditioners contained a large amount of vinegar. This made it possible for you to wash your hair and then immediately:

    a. wash your windows

    b. eat a large Caesar Salad

    c. de-scale your coffeemaker

    d. take a douche

    * d. plus a,b, and c if you were ambidextrous.

2. Pancake make-up looked best when applied directly on the face and THEN carefully blended with:

    a. a spatula

    b. a damp sponge mop

    c. a Brillo pad

    d. a Sunbeam Electric Mixer

    * d. set on "puree."

3. Any cosmetic sold today must be regulated and approved by:

    a. the FDA

    b. the SPCA

    c. the FCC

    d. Cher

    * d. the ultimate Infomercial authority.

4. Before the advent of microchip technology where molecular substances are added to thicken mascara, what kind of chips were used?

   a. chocolate

   b. potato

   c. buffalo

   d. poker

   * a,b,and c . It also doubled as mighty tasty fudge.

5. Before it was discovered that Retin A was an excellent anti-wrinkle cream, by what primitive means did we accomplish exfoliation?

   a. with a red hot sunlamp

   b. using a Honey N' Ajax scrub

   c. applying bathroom decals and peeling them off

   d. with our Dad's electric sander

   * any of the above plus a shot of novocaine would do 'ya.

CHAPTER 6

SHAVING IN THE FIFTIES:
IT WAS THE PITS

THE 50's BATHING SUIT: A REAL BONER

Remember the traditional one-piece bathing suit of the 50's? It had a little pleated skirt which reached mid-thigh and lots of draping to conceal the bustline. In fact, nowadays, this style could be worn to church. These suits were so modest, they covered more territory than the Yukon. In fact they hid womens' saddlebags so well, that cellulite went virtually undiscovered until the late 60's.

They also had built-in shelf-style bras, molded with *formica* contour pads strong enough to launch the Space Shuttle. Furthermore, all of the suits in those days had built-in rubber girdles. Even if you weighed only 75 pounds soaking wet, a girdle under a bathing suit was a must. Remember, muscle tone was not an important part of anybody's physique back then. So to give our bodies some kind of shape, the 50's bathing suits had about two dozen "bones" sewn into them—and if any of them broke, the suit would require a total body cast.

ELECTRIC GROOMING:
IN THE NICK OF TIME

Because the bathing suits of the 50's covered about 75% of your body, not much prep work had to be done. However, for what little trimming we needed, our favorite feminine grooming aid, the Princess Electric Shaver was the only way to go. Packaged in a cream-colored carrying case with a pink satin lining, this dreamy appliance was found on every teenage girl's vanity table. It was the ultimate feminine ritual to disappear into the bathroom on Saturday afternoons and plug in. Getting a "buzz on" in the 50's was a whole different experience than it is today.

However, shaving was not always a breeze. Remember, this was in the days before Victor Kiam bought the company, so the electric razor was not exactly "state of the art." The dull shaving head pinched our armpits and nicked our legs, leaving a two inch wide razor burn in its wake. But we persevered! No one would be caught dead with unsightly underarm hair or calf stubble, except the gals on the bowling team who could grate cheese on their legs.

BATHING SUITS OF THE 90's:
THE BARE TRUTH

Leafing through a catalogue of today's bathing suits, you would swear you were looking at an issue of Playboy and not the good old Speigel's. Even the one-piece styles are copied from your basic sling-shot. Page after page proudly displays beach bunnies wearing creations slit from the hips to the armpits and bikinis revealing more butt cleavage than a Sumo wrestler.

Others have see-through slashes, cut-outs, and peek-a-boo netting showing parts of the anatomy previously reserved only for medical textbooks. The gal wearing one of these is certainly making her own personal fashion statement— which says:

"Hey guys, basically I'm easy."

Any woman who can successfully carry off one of these skimpy suits has to have two prime attributes: she must be anorexic and more hairless than a Mexican Chihuahua. And to achieve that "hairless" look, we have to remove roughly 2/3 of our body hair. This process is not only time consuming but can be excruciatingly painful, as well. However, modern science has elevated the problem of hair removal to a state of the art technology which is accomplished by choosing any of the following torture devices:

THE RAZOR BLADE: SCRAPE AND TAPE

Shaving the bikini area with a razor blade requires you to follow the same protocol as nurses do when they're prepping a patient for surgery. You'll need plenty of antiseptic shaving cream, an arsenal of razor blades, and 60 feet of sterile surgical bandage. Remember, your razor will be venturing into territory unchartered by the Gillette Company,

VICTOR KIAM, WHERE ARE YOU?

so proceed with extreme caution. We're talking about places that are not only hard to find, but nobody would want to look for them anyway. But these bathing suits cover NOTHING and SHOW EVERYTHING, so it just has to be done.

Now, if you do accidentally cut yourself in this sensitive area, don't panic. Just apply direct pressure to the wound by sitting down on a hard surface for at least 5 minutes.

THE BIKINI WAX: DRIP AND RIP

The bikini wax is often touted as a proven method of hair removal. Yes, it's proven to be about the most painful experience a woman can endure next to an unanesthetized episiotomy. It is prudent to undertake this procedure with at least 50 mg. of Percodan and Demerol on board, and a backup of IV morphine. Many women prefer an epidural anesthetic which, although very effective, makes it impossible to leave the house for eight hours, because of the total loss of motor control in your legs.

The procedure is basically quite simple. Heat the wax to the temperature of a well fired pizza oven and pour it on. The tricky part is in trying to remain conscious long enough to rip the whole thing off once it has dried. And if you don't want your neighbors calling 911 all afternoon, it might be best to either do this in a sound-proof room or borrow your dog's muzzle.

ELECTRIC COIL HAIR REMOVAL: FRY AND CRY

The new electric coil gadgets claim to remove the hair completely from it's root, leaving you hairless for weeks. And even though it's advertised as a system of "painless" hair removal, they do come with a rawhide strap to bite down on. What they don't tell you is that this coil requires a 220 volt outlet to handle the power surge. Because of the high voltage, they're standard issue in all State Penitentiaries as a backup system to the "chair."

The recommended use is for legs only, because any use above the waist could produce the same result as electro-shock therapy. Then you would forget *who you are*, much less that you need a shave.

One good point is that the discomfort level is minimal compared to a waxing— let's say, about the same as pulling your hairs out one by one with a tweezer. The advantage here is that re-growth is slow. When the hair does begin to grow back in a few weeks, it has *mutated* to the consistency of a Brillo pad. Some women find that this new growth is just a bit too thick for the coil to handle. So for their next shave, they have to use a Black and Decker hedge trimmer.

DEPILATORIES: SPREAD AND SHED

Most women agree that depilatories are by far the easiest and quickest hair removal method.

BLACK & DECKER: THE FINEST
IN FEMININE PRODUCTS

Following the three-step procedure on the box, you apply, wait 15 minutes, then rinse off the unwanted hair in the shower. The only other thing you'll need is your own personal plumber on call 24 hours a day to keep your drain unclogged. Keep in mind that you're going to be shedding more hair in 15 minutes than your pet Collie does all summer.

Most manufacturers advise against the use of depilatories for underarms. The chemicals may be a bit too harsh for the delicate skin in this area, causing severe rash and painful swelling. If a bad reaction does happen, chances are a woman may find that she is unable to shave for up to six months. Until then, she'll have to find an alternative solution—like learning to cornrow her underarm hair.

LETTING IT ALL HANG OUT: NOT

After you're all prepped for the premiere showing of your scanty new bathing suit, the next obstacle is learning how to sit, lie, or lounge and keep what little is covered from falling out. You know, "hanging out without really hanging out." It is not easy to lie discreetly on a lounge chair wearing a bathing suit that begins at the tailbone with legholes extending to the waist. Keep in mind that this bathing suit is going to provide you with less basic coverage than an Art Linkletter health insurance plan.

One false move could prove very embarrassing. It's tricky but not impossible. Remember, Johnny Weismuller maintained his PG rating while swinging on vines wearing little more than you are; so you can do it.

POSITION STATEMENTS:
AVOIDING ANGLE DANGLE

You will have to remember that certain positions in these suits will display your flesh at it's worst angles. For example, lying flat on your back will virtually quadruple the area of your thighs. So avoid this posture while at the beach. You don't want any well-meaning Save The Whales groups attempting to coax you out to sea.

Special attention should be paid to keeping your breasts from falling out while wearing halter top suits. Unlike the 50's when the suits had built-in bras molded from bullet-proof tupperware, the present day suits are constructed with measly one-inch straps. They barely cover the bust and provide less support than one of Truman Capote's jock straps. Keep in mind that the laws of gravity apply to the breast as well as the apple.

Historical Point of Interest: *Sir Issac Newton found this out in his not-so-famous sequel experiment in which he utilized a sling-shot, a hard apple, and his Indian girlfriend, Princess Wounded Hooter.*

The point is that even a simple act like twisting from the waist can cause all hell to break loose. There's just no way to discreetly remove a boob that's been caught between your lounge slats. So be careful of your moves unless, of course, you are attempting to make one on some hunky lifeguard— then go for it!

SUITS WITH AN ATTITUDE: GETTING CHEEKY

For the extremely brave woman with a perfect body, you will most likely be dying to try one of the latest new thong bikinis. These suits have the thin string in the rear that looks like butt floss. Most women have spent their whole lives trying to keep their underpants *out of there*, so why anybody would want to wear a suit like this boggles the mind. It's like there is NO coverage there. But guys love to see womens' butts. So you better make sure you have no excess hair, pimples, or blemishes of any kind to spoil your appearance. You must put your BEST buttface forward!

It goes without saying that firm buttock muscles are a must for these suits. You will have to spend several months working on those "gleuts" in the gym. You'll know you're pumped up enough to look sensational wearing a thong bikini when you can catch a Nolan Ryan fastball between your cheeks.

It doesn't take much maneuvering to lose one of these suits in or out of the water. When you wear this suit to the beach, unfortunately swimming is out of the question. The thrashing undertow can pull off the bikini bottom faster than your honey's upper toe. But you can explore a lot of other activities just laying on the beach meditating with your guy. Get away from the physical and get into the metaphysical plane. The longer you lay there, the greater the chance that you'll be having an out-of-bikini experience real soon.

77

QUIZ 6

1. The torpedo-tipped bras under the 50's bathing suits were molded to make the breasts come to points. While swimming, they also had the added function of:

   a. spearing fish

   b. acting as a rudder

   c. cutting through icebergs

   d. busting everyones' inner tubes

   * a. a couple of tunas could fit on each D cup.

2. What one word is associated more than any other with the thong bikini:

   a. sexy

   b. European

   c. daring

   d. hemorrhoids

   * d. just ask any woman who wears one.

3. In order to be well-groomed, the girls of the 50's who couldn't afford Princess Electric shavers used:

   a. potato peelers

   b. hedge clippers

   c. styling gel

   d. knee socks

* c nobody can fault well-coiffed legs.

4. The only thing more revealing than a thong bikini is:

    a. going topless

    b. a gynecological exam

    c. J. Edgar Hoover's closet

    d. a hospital gown

    * c. may be revealed on "Geraldo" soon.

5. As an alternative to a bikini wax you might choose:

    a. depilatories

    b. electrolysis

    c. bathing suits with a skirt

    d. bathing suits with fur trim

    * d. and naturally, the fur of choice is beaver.

CHAPTER 7

FIFTIES FITNESS: WE CAME OUT SMOKIN'

50's EXERCISE: A REAL DRAG

In the 50's, exercise was pretty much limited to getting up and changing the channel, reaching for the cheese doodles, then taking deep drags on your cigarette. The most rigorous sport of the day was ping-pong, which hardly produced the popular exploding bicep look of today. However, it afforded little chance of serious injury except for an occasional groin pull for the gals who reached down to tie their sneakers or for those guys who foolishly attempted to play the game without wearing a jockstrap.

One reason why we were all so weak and pasty looking was because everybody smoked in those days. The only part of our bodies showing any color at all was our fingers and teeth, which were brownish-yellow from nicotine stains. Remember, we're talking about the days when the Surgeon General was still a four pack-a-day man, himself. And the cigarettes in those days were so full of tar and nicotine, even the *cigarette machines* got cancer. So the main exercise for smokers was flicking our Bic's. Anything more strenuous might cause you to barf up a lung or something.

COLLEGE SMOKING: THE VARSITY DRAG

During the college years, we moved on to a new smoking territory called Marlboro Country. These were rugged times. Life got tough. To study for "all-nighters," we were armed with our lighters in one hand and our highlighters in the other.

Everyone tried to emulate their idol, the most popular of all the Marlboro poster men, Tom Selleck. All of us girls fantasized about lighting up with Tom—in the saddle, of course. Thinking about that scene, we'd lie in our beds puffing and also huffing a lot. After "lights out" at midnight, there was more coughing and wheezing heard than during the entire filming of "Camille."

ORAL GRATIFICATION: IT SUCKS

However within the next decade, smoking became identified as the major cause of our nation's most serious health problems like cancer, heart disease, emphysema, and bad breath.

Our smoking habit finally expired along with many of our smokin' heroes like Bogey, Bette Davis, and Gary Cooper—who were always seen with a cigarette dangling provocatively between their lips. Oral gratification was replaced with a new **Anal Retentive Generation** led by wholesome types like Oral Roberts, Orel Hershiser, and Oral Redenbacher— who incidentally, never had anything dangling from their lips or anyplace else, for that matter.

SMOKING IN THE NINETIES:
A COVERT OPERATION

In the 90's, smokers are about as socially acceptable as serial killers. Banned from restaurants, public buildings, restrooms, airports and more, about the only place a smoker can go to light up is the same place he went when he was a teenager: behind his garage. Young adults are especially fanatic anti-smoking crusaders, and most will refuse to date anyone who smokes.

Nowadays, any guy in a singles bar trying to pick up a gal with some stupid line while simultaneously blowing smoke in her face, will be subjected to this standard retort:

"Listen fellow, if I really wanted to shorten my life, I'd date you."

UNCOVERING YOUR BODY:
AN ACT OF TERRORISM

Today we have become a nation of non-smokers obsessed with achieving the lean, muscular hard-bodies of finely-tuned athletes— and breasts like Sybil Danning's. But transforming a 50's ex-smoker's endomorphic physique capable of an imminent "flabbalanche" into one of pulsating pumpitude is no small task!

The first step is by far the toughest part— assessing what you've got. You're going to have to take a hard, cold look at your naked body in a full length mirror. Keep in mind that this alone can be a terrifying experience. You're going to discover more lumps than you do in your mattress and count more rolls than you'd see in a deli.

Some of you may become particularly distressed to discover that the cute little puppy tattoo on your butt has grown to the size of a water buffalo. Or worse yet, the perky little rose on your left breast has grown a six-inch stem over the last few years.

BREAST CHECK: GETTING THE LEAD OUT

Turning sideways to check out the state of our breasts can be a real bummer. They will probably look about as firm as last week's bratwurst and will have assumed the same shape, too. To be truthful, nowadays most of us are wearing a size 36 **Long** bra. To measure breast firmness, women have consulted the best experts in the business. Of course, these are the knowledgeable folks at Cosmo Magazine. Their famous boob test, "MEASURING YOUR BREAST I.Q.: How Does Yours Stack Up?" has been performed by millions of anxious women over the decade.

Ready? Here goes. Place a pencil under your bust. If it immediately falls out— good news— the breast has still retained it's youthful firmness. If the pencil stays in— bad news— you've lost muscle tone which is causing the obvious sag. And we've all seen some sorry examples of this. There's no sight more pathetic than an old stripper who is sweeping the floor with her tassels. But the majority of women under 30 find that even after three pencils, none

HMM... NOT QUITE AS FIRM
AS THEY USED TO BE

have fallen out. However, the sad truth for those of us over 40 is that our breasts are not only retaining a gross of pencils, but could easily accommodate a couple of tree trunks too.

THE PERSONAL TRAINER: JOCKSTRAP JOCKIES

When we finally reach a point where we are thoroughly disgusted with the state of our bodies, women will head straight for the gym. And why not turn this into the most pleasant experience possible? To do this, sign up with a hunky male workout coach— the thick inflatable type of guy who teaches one-on-one weight training and really makes you sweat buckets. Now, most women rightfully feel that if they wanted to sweat this much there should be some sex involved. But remember, these guys spend most of their time admiring their own butts. So these buff guys are really not your best bet for a great "roll-in-the-hay." You'd be better off with the horse— besides, it'd have a higher I.Q.

WOMEN WHO PUMP IRON: BUT DON'T DATE MUCH

And what's the deal with those hardcore women who are into pumping iron? They look like they go to the bathroom standing up. These babes have taken so many steroids that when they pump iron, they don't grunt, they whinny. Their main goal in life is attaining the buffed-up bicep look of Linda Hamilton

MISS AMERICA
TURNING INTO THE INCREDIBLE HULK

in "Terminator II." You'll never catch one of them experiencing underarm jiggle while firing off a round on their Uzi's. But even though their look would not make them a prime candidate as one of the trampy females on "Studs," at least they could fill in for one of the guys if he didn't show up.

So if the American Gladiator look is your thing, then go for it. But if you are content to remain looking like one of your own species, you should settle on a tamer form of exercise— like male bashing or even aerobics.

AEROBICS CLASSES: BUTT BUSTERS

One of the most popular features of a health club is the aerobics classes. A word of caution here. Get there early and stake out your floor space. The "regulars" in these classes become very territorial and once they have picked out their "spot," they'll viciously attack anything within two feet of it.

To say the floors are hard is the understatement of the year.

Most health clubs install carpet pads woven from fibers of solid concrete. They could wear out the shocks on a semi in a matter of hours. Keep this in mind, because you will be adding two new words to your vocabulary: *shin splints.*

Although aerobics is generally considered to be a relatively safe activity, it isn't entirely without risk. Anytime you have a room filled to capacity with frantically bouncing overweight women, there is always a chance you could get severely flogged by someone's behind. Or, go deaf from the heavy metal music which is cranked up to ear-bleeding intensity for 60 minutes. Also, aerobics classes are notorious for filling the room to capacity. This gives them the unique distinction of packing more lard per square inch than a can of Crisco.

Be careful to choose a class appropriate to your level of ability. Because of the tremendous amount of jumping you do in the advanced high impact classes, the degree of difficulty is measured by the number of **Depends** you'll go through in a 45 minute period.

AEROBICS CHIC: THE CUTTING EDGE

You must be sure to appear only in the trendiest of aerobics outfits or else everyone will know the last time you exercised was with Jack LaLanne in 1957. The current fad in aerobics "chic" is stretchy spandex cut high on the hip with a thong butt strap. Many carry warning labels advising the manufacturers' limits on the number of deep knee bends which can be safely undertaken before you'll execute a partial episiotomy on yourself.

If you are "top-heavy," as an added precaution, keep an exercise mat underneath you at all times. A wildly bouncing D Cup breast has been the cause of many a woman going down from a self-inflicted TKO to the chin. Take note also of just how high the workout suits are cut on the hips. They are not made to be worn with your dorky old underpants

JOG 'N FLOG

underneath. Even if you try to roll them up out of sight, it's a sure bet that with each successive kick they'll ride down until they're sticking out somewhere around your knees. And ditto for your maxipads. When these inch down, you'll have a hard time explaining why you need to wear one around your thighs.

RULES FOR THE FLOOR

Rule One— be prepared to pass out.

Rule Two— never watch the clock.

Your body will subtly tell you when 5 minutes have passed by inflicting shortness of breath, dizziness, and severe chest pain. If, on the 465th repetition of "Rover's Revenge" you are getting rabid, and your thighs burst into flame— congratulations— you went for the "burn" and got it!

Caution: During the Jumping Jacks, the floor may get slick from "accidents" perpetrated by 40-year-old bladders. Be Prepared. Wear Reebok "pumps," they also double as flotation devices.

The last 10 minutes are devoted to "cool down" and stretching exercises. It's your time to relax, doze off, and forget all about your daily chores. Unfortunately, the sound produced from multiple female joints snapping, crackling, and popping will probably remind you that you forgot to give your kid his Rice Krispies this morning.

QUIZ

1. In the 50's, one cigarette contained the same amount of tar as you would find in:

   a. 10 of the low-tar cigarettes of today

   b. 20 of the low-tar cigarettes of today

   c. a box of Havana cigars

   d. the La Brea Pits

   * *d. plus the Indy 500 racetrack.*

2. Many of the muscle-bound trainers found in today's gyms are addicted to:

   a. steroids

   b. mega-vitamins

   c. sex

   d. mirrors

   * *c and d. sex with themselves in front of mirrors.*

3. One thing that women body-builders are assured of never having is:

   a. cellulite

   b. heart disease

   c. a bust

   d. a date

   * *c or d unless they pay for them.*

4. Protein powder supplements are necessary for the body to manufacture:

    a. muscle tissue

    b. amino acids

    c. strong bones

    d. gallstones

    * *d. one bowling ball-sized gallstone per tablespoon.*

5. "Buns of Steel" is a popular workout video made by:

    a. the Bisquick Company

    b. the AFL-CIO chapter in Pittsburgh

    c. Jimmy The Greek

    d. the American Hip Replacement Foundation

    * *a. featuring Julia Child doing all the demonstrations.*

CHAPTER 8

FLYING IN THE FIFTIES: GERIATRIC AIRLINES

THE FIFTIES FLIGHT CREW: CHRONOLOGICALLY CHALLENGED

Remember when Bogey let Ingrid Bergman board that prop plane without him on that foggy night in "Casablanca?" He was no fool. He didn't go with her because he knew it was suicide to fly in that old rattletrap. And we knuckleheads of that generation sat and swooned because we assumed he was doing it out of honor. Get real. In those days, you were about as safe using one of those planes as you were using the rhythm method.

More than a decade later in the 50's, we got the same crew who flew on Ingrid's original flight. The age requirement of stewardesses in those days was simply listed as *post-menopausal.* How old were they? Well, most of them were so old they referred to Lindbergh as "Chuck." And because of their advanced ages, after they demonstrated how to use the oxygen masks, most of them kept theirs on during the entire flight.

50's PASSENGERS: FLYING HIGH

In the 50's when you flew, only one class was available—steerage. Also, smoking was encouraged in all cabin locations. In fact, the crew was instructed to hand out small samplers of cigarettes to the passengers, and the stews lit up along with everyone else at takeoff to make them feel "at home."

Alcoholic beverages were not only free but freely distributed around the cabin. Everybody got a big kick from watching the captain staggering around the cockpit swigging 'em down while wearing his bunny suit and aviator goggles. The passengers had such a ball, often the captain eliminated the two drink minimum sign. Many times the flying party got so loud and rowdy it was impossible to hear the safety precautions being sung by the cabin attendants. It didn't matter anyway, because by that point, nobody really cared if they lived or died.

50's FLIGHT MOTTO: SHAKE IT UP BABY

The deafening roar from the engines of those old prop planes was certainly nothing like the quiet hum of today's DC-10 jet engines—even when they're falling off the wings. The vibrations from those antique propellers were so jarring, the elderly passengers frequently lost their dentures upon takeoff, while others lost their cookies.

The normal cruising altitude was 1,000 feet. This was great for the kids on board, who were able to play travel games like reading license plates or

HOW HIGH CAN YOU FLY?

counting cows across the country. And they made so many stops, some passengers got off in their driveways. Kids got special treatment in those days. The ever solicitous flight attendants of the 50's initiated the charming practice of pinning wings on each child—which came from renegade pigeons sucked into the engines.

IN-FLIGHT AMENITIES: THE SURVIVAL KIT

Because these aircraft were manufactured without cabin speakers, the captain and his crew shouted their words of welcome from the cockpit. There were two things we didn't like to hear: *One:* When the captain introduced himself and added that he would be retiring at the end of the flight and *Two:* When they rang the bell and issued the warning: "Fasten your seatbelts, we're in for a bumpy flight."

All the passengers cringed after these words, because we all remembered that after Bette Davis said the same thing in "All About Eve," her life went straight into the toilet. And we sure didn't want to end up in the same place after being tossed around the cabin for an hour.

Climate control was a concept yet to be discovered. Most of the time, we sat there and froze. Even the flight attendants, who all looked like Aunt Bea with an attitude, wore longjohns under their uniforms while moving about the icy cabin. The old birds weren't insulated very well, and for that matter, neither were the planes. In fact, there was more gooseflesh to be seen than in all of Frank Perdue's factories combined.

LANDING PROCEDURES:
A WING AND A PRAYER

We were told that in the likely event the fuel ran low, in order to stay aloft, we would have to jettison anything of no use to us. This was when you witnessed many women pushing their husbands towards the nearest exit. A few minutes later when the captain yelled back it was time to land, this was the cue to open your window and throw out your cigarettes before donning the supplied crash helmet.

The flight attendants advised you again of the five emergency exits, including the **really big one** that would be created upon impact. We braced ourselves as the pilot nosed down for the standard Kamikaze landing. Big-breasted women had a distinct advantage because as the plane dove down at 2G's, their bras filled with air and floated above their heads like parachutes cushioning their impact at touch down. And if it was a water landing, they were able to float three hours longer than anyone else.

NEUROSIS IN THE 90's:
FEAR OF BOARDING

By today's standards, this scenario seems tame. Now we have to worry about a whole raft of catastrophes like loose engine bolts, striking personnel, and worst of all—non-refundable airline tickets. The only reason they will give a refund nowadays is for a death in the family. And even at that, for proof you

"ARE YOU, BY CHANCE, PASSENGER 57?"

have to supply a copy of the death certificate, a copy of the malpractice suit filed against the surgeon, and a certified photograph of the deceased standing next to Elvis.

Another thing to worry about is all the terrorists and impressionable bombers who have been watching videos of "Airport I, II, and III" all afternoon at the terminal. So if you happen to be put in seat #56, and the swarthy guy next to you is wearing a big name tag saying "Passenger 57," head for the nearest exit.

AIRLINE FOOD: BAKED SALMON-ELLA

Even if you successfully beat the odds of being killed from any of the above, the airline food will surely do you in. Instead of trying to make that gross food appear palatable by serving it with fancy garnishes and good linen, they would save themselves big bucks by serving it directly in the barf bags— since that's where it usually ends up anyway. One entree routinely served on domestic flights is the "Roast Boeuf Du Exxon." This dish consists of a sliced portion of bologna having an iridescent shimmer strongly suggestive of an oil slick.

Also, the crew is trained to deceptively sidestep any questions concerning the origin of the main course. You might get a hint of this practice if you foolishly ask, "Stewardess, is this fish fresh?" She'll reply, "Yes, we have a net hanging off the wing." But the airline has become quite savvy in handling the consequences of any dish they serve. Immediately after it is placed on your tray, the overhead information light flashes:

This flashing advisory is immediately upgraded to "Condition Red: Barf Bag Overload." For those lucky enough to negotiate shoving past the other 80 passengers waiting in line and make it to the bathroom first, there is another flashing universal symbol above the toilet bowl:

IN-FLIGHT ENTERTAINMENT: DE-ICING THE PASSENGERS

But take heart. The airline intends to make full restitution to all survivors on board by proudly presenting it's first un-cut adult movie with it's own personalized rating of **Rx**. Kids are given blindfolds and earplugs while the adults are only too happy to watch:

"Sex Starved Stewardesses Layover In Scranton."

The two hour feature is simultaneously accompanied by the latest airline advisory flashing intermittently:

In the likely event that the projector overheats from the rise in body heat generated from the passengers, the flight crew is happy to act out the remaining scenes LIVE for your viewing pleasure. Captain Kirk "Bud" Schmooz will take the part of "Manley F. Buttcheeks," steel pipefitter, "Lola" the love-starved flight tramp is ably played by first cabin attendant Maureen DuMammary. "Innocent Boy" is played by cabin gopher Benjamin Gaye and "Rover the Wonder Dog" is played by Captain Kirk's own German Shepherd, Horneigh. Incidentally, Ms. DuMammary received a special in-flight award for best performance by an actress in a non-speaking role.

As you sit back and enjoy the show, do not be alarmed by the increased amount of turbulence. The crew will announce that it is being auto-generated by the large number of passengers themselves, who are really getting into the performance.

So relax and don't worry. The only other possible danger would be an air traffic controller who was dumped that morning by his overweight/transvestite/cross-dressing/serial killer/lover, and who decides to take out his frustration by forcing the plane to circle Poland for six hours. But that is a very remote possibility. Chances are the airline food will get you first.

QUIZ 8

1. Upgrading from coach to first class is made easy by most airlines if you are willing to trade in your frequent flyer miles and:

   a. your firstborn child

   b. your IRA

   c. a year's salary

   d. your American citizenship

   * any of the above will get you a first class ticket from Cleveland to Dayton.

2. Tampering with smoke detectors in the plane's bathroom could get you:

   a. thrown in jail

   b. a $1,000 fine

   c. your only chance to smoke a cigarette

   d. electrocuted

   * d. if you are taking a whizz while doing it.

3. The best way to have sex on an airplane without being caught is:

   a. for both of you to sneak into the lavatory

   b. do it in your carry-on steamer trunk

   c. do it by yourself under the blanket

   d. illuminate the call button for the stewardess

   * d. this insures you will have at least an

hour before she shows up.

4. In the event of a water landing, your best chance for survival is by:

    a. inflating the life preserver AFTER you de-plane

    b. inflating your bra BEFORE you de-plane

    c. removing your Depend for better buoyancy

    d. using your seat cushion as a flotation device: but do NOT smell it before or after de-planing

    * *d. an oxygen mask will substantially help your chances for survival.*

5. In an effort to gain more business, many airlines are now offering meals that:

    a. won't require lawsuit insurance

    b. are low in cholesterol AND Salmonella

    c. aren't runny on the inside

    d. are pre-chewed for your convenience

    * *all of the above. But when they make them EDIBLE too, they'll have it made.*

MONTEZUMA STRIKES AGAIN

CHAPTER 9

FOREIGN TRAVEL:
ALL ROADS LEAD
TO BAD RESTROOMS

50's TRAVEL:
AROUND THE BLOCK IN EIGHTY MINUTES

About the farthest place a kid in the fifties would travel to was across town on a Sunday afternoon motor trip with the folks. And you were forced to wear your "Sunday Clothes" to go visit some despised or boring relative.

Inevitably, Dad's car was one of those lame 50's Pontiacs that was so underpowered, when you pushed in the cigarette lighter, the car slowed down. We were definitely not the jet-setting seasoned travelers like the kids of today. In those days if we crossed the town line, we got jet lag. Plus, the change of water way across town upset our systems. If you were one of those kids who had a hankering for more exotic locations, you had to find them in the pages of the National Geographic— amongst the bare native breasts, of course.

By contrast, today's kids have logged more frequent flier miles by the time they're 16 than the whole country did in the fifties. Teenagers routinely travel to both U.S. coasts, to Europe, or places like Hawaii and Mexico for their spring vacations. While their folks considered their bus tour through the Amish country the highlight of their lives, today's kids feel deprived if they're not totally blitzed on frozen daiquiris in Aruba over spring break.

MEXICAN VACATION:
THE ACCIDENTS of TOURISTS

If you're planning to have some fun in the sun in any of Mexico's resorts, like beautiful **Playa Del Diarrhea**, read on for tips on how to prevent it from turning into the dreaded Vacation In Hell.

1. Take a course of preventive antibiotics—even before boarding the plane.

It's so *gringo* to forget where you are. Throwing caution to the wind, you'll wolf down large quantities of fresh fruit, burritos, tacos, local water, and ensalada—acting like wild and loco *Americanos*. But just remember that the Great Momtezuma WILL get his revenge, and usually at some ungodly hour like 3 a.m. This is when you suddenly awake in your hotel room believing that a band of *hombres* is doing the *flamenco* on your stomach.

2. Take plenty of Pepto-Bismol and reading material with you.

When *tourista* hits, you'll be suffering with such severe cramps that there is no other recourse but to race to the bathroom. This is where the reading material comes in; you'll be staying in there for the next three days. If you're lucky, the *toilettas* will have

a small window, and you can still catch sight of a few glorious sunsets, some windsurfers, and possibly reach out and touch an occasional parasailer blown off course. By the fourth day, you will emerge on rubbery legs with a body so dehydrated, you can get a gig with the California Raisins.

3. Pack a pair of precautionary black rubber pants for future outings.

When you finally recover and attempt your first real meal in three days, avoid foods like spicy *chimichangas*. Be prudent and order up the intestinally pampering dishes like a bowl of mushy *pollo* and rice with an Immodium D cream sauce. However, don't be surprised if it barely clears your esophagus before you find yourself in *el deepo manuro*.

Leaping out of your chair, you will beat a hasty retreat for... that's right, your old buddy *los toiletta*. Try not to knock down any *caballeros* in your way. Your whole body will be drenched in a cold sweat from the exertion of trying to hold back the inevitable explosion. The patrons will be snickering and mumbling things to each other like "*El Gringo has Jalapeno blowout.*"

4. Even before you order, check to see if the bathroom is "occupado" and make sure it has a good supply of toilet paper.

Be advised: in your haste, if you happen to knock some *senora* off the toilet seat, you could get 10 years in the Mexican slammer. Once you hit the seat, brace yourself for the deafening blast which will

MORE LOMOTIL... STAT!

rock the building to it's very adobe foundation. Don't be surprised if the porcelain bowl cracks in half. The force behind this blast will be about equal to standing in back of Raymond Burr in a refried bean factory.

And if that isn't humiliating enough, if there is no toilet paper, you'll be wildly rifling through your purse or pockets for a piece of Kleenex. When you find none, you'll lower your goals and look for a Toni home-perm end paper or an old gum wrapper, or the leaves from a chewed up Havana cigar. And if you come up empty, what you end up doing will definitely rank up there as THE most desperate moment of your life. Were Mr. Whipple around, you would promise him things he never dared to imagine in exchange for one sheet of Charmin.

BATHROOM RESERVATIONS:
THE PAUSE THAT REFRESHES

Intestinal precautions should not be limited only to Mexico. When planning a European vacation, there are other problems of this nature that need to be addressed. Be smart and arm yourself with medications to cover every intestinal malady known on the Continent— and prepare for the Incontinent, too. Here's some mandatory intestinal tips:

1. Stock up on those Berlitz tapes that teach you how to say "Where's the bathroom?" in 16 languages including Arabic— in case of a terrorist hijacking.

2. For treating European diarrhea, (a much higher class of this ailment) pack a Vuitton steamer trunk filled with Lomotil, Bactrim, Pepto-Bismol, and six cases of 12-ply lotioned toilet tissue. For problems of the opposite nature, pack ExLax, Ducolax, Hailey's MO, Feenamint, and spansules of time released bowel explosives. This will probably get you declared as an "International Pharmacy". a.k.a "*Farmacia Internazionale*" by customs officials who will then duly rubber stamp your forehead as such.

But wear it proudly, like that camera hanging around your neck. Remember you have a time-honored image to uphold: "The Ugly American."

3. Book rooms having an adjoining bathroom with NO door. Try to get one with a view of the city's cathedrals and monuments (this may be your only chance to see them). And, whenever possible, reserve pool lounges closest to the public restrooms. Don't give a foreign government's EPA the opportunity to hold you responsible for creating a major urine slick in their swimming pool.

THE TEN CARDINAL RULES
OF INTERNATIONAL BOWEL DIPLOMACY

Whatever else you do, these rules are imperative for any traveler to memorize. They have been advocated by the State Department to save you from creating a messy international **incident**, (or hopefully, one in your own pants.)

1. Never dance the *Tarantella* wearing a white suit after eating a quart of salsa.

2. If you eat *pasta fagiole*, make sure it's followed by a Pepto-Bismol chaser.

3. If your bowels haven't moved in 10 days, you may be declared **legally dead** by a foreign government.

4. You have had too much Lomotil when you've slept through a two week hostage crisis—and you were the hostage.

5. Never walk the "silent halls of the Prado" after ingesting a quart of lentils.

6. Avoid genuflecting in the Sistine Chapel after a dinner of fried calamari.

7. Never share a public phone booth with a British citizen after an afternoon in a pub eating kidney pie and swilling ale.

8. If you do have an "accident" in a New Delhi open market, DO NOT blame it on the sacred cow waiting in line ahead of you.

9. For your own personal safety and for others, wear a pair of stiff ski boots when executing a deep knee bend over the hole in a Chinese out-house.

10. For the sake of national security, never wander into a demilitarized zone where a cease fire has been declared for at least 12 hours after eating anything containing cabbage.

NEVER DANCE THE TARANTELLA
IN A WHITE SUIT

QUIZ 9

1. When treating a severe case of Montezuma's Revenge, doctors recommend that you avoid:

   a. solid foods for 72 hours

   b. using their restrooms

   c. making any sudden moves

   d. white underpants

   * c. making any sudden moves in d. white underpants.

2. In England, everyone refers to the toilet as the:

   a. "loo"

   b. "Fergie"

   c. "bowl"

   d. "Camilla-Parker Bowl"

   * d. also refers to a Polo Tournament sponsored by Tampax.

3. A hearty belch after ingesting a great Italian meal is:

   a. considered a compliment to the chef

   b. considered to be boorish by all

   c. a turn on to any Italian male

   d. boorish—but a hell of a lot better than farting

   * c. picking your teeth or nose is also.

4. Not tipping an Iraqi waiter after dinner is:

    a. punishable by death

    b. reason enough for the country to declare war

    c. going to get you castrated

    d. just cause to launch a Scud missile at the U.S.

    * *all of the above, plus hosting a dinner for Saddam.*

5. An old Arabic proverb says "He who lives on beans alone..."

    a. lives alone

    b. walks with the camels

    c. walks awfully fast

    d. dies by exploding

    * *d. and leaves a hell of a mess for the cleaning lady.*

EPILOGUE

Looking back, I don't think that anything in the 50's was really all that different than it is in the 90's. It's just that now, everything is more *out in the open.* This not only goes for our attitudes about sex but our underwear, too. In the old days, we confessed our sexual transgressions to a priest, and now we broadcast them to millions on daytime T.V. talk shows. And while we used to wear our bullet bras under our sweaters, now we wear them *instead* of the sweaters.

After the country made the collective decision in the 60's to "let it all hang out," we're spending the 90's toning and oiling what's hanging out there. To accomplish this, we had to trade in our hula-hoops for thighmasters, our bicycles for life-cycles, and our roller skates for roller blades. There's no doubt that this is a much healthier era, physically and psychologically. I don't think there is anyone left who would want to go back to our unhealthy, undisciplined habits of the 50's— is there? And while we're thinking it over, let's have a cup of coffee, a chocolate-covered doughnut, and a cigarette.

BIOGRAPHY

Jan King is the author of three national best selling humor books, "Hormones From Hell," "Husbands From Hell," and "It's Better To Be Over The Hill Than Under It." She has appeared nationally on many TV talk shows including "Jenny Jones," "Jerry Springer," "Montel Williams," and "Sonya Live." She appears regularly on the Detroit based T.V. talk show "Company" and recently made an appearance on the national Canadian talk show, "Dini Petty."

She would love to go on many more talk shows, but refuses to stab anybody to death with her own Killer Bra in order to become a "qualified" guest— a small flesh wound, maybe.

Jan makes her home in California with her publisher/husband Mark, her son Philip, and three pet Poodle skirts.

TITLES BY CCC PUBLICATIONS

— NEW BOOKS —

KILLER BRAS And Other
Hazards Of The 50's.....................................$5.95
by Jan King
HOW TO ENTERTAIN PEOPLE YOU HATE.......$4.95
by Ari Alexandra Boulanger
LIFE'S MOST EMBARRASSING MOMENTS $4.95
by Steve Berman
THE BOTTOM HALF $4.95
by S. D. Williams
NEVER A DULL CARD $5.95
by John Carfi & Cliff Carle
WORK SUCKS! $5.95
by Bob Glickman
THE UGLY TRUTH ABOUT MEN $5.95
by Tom Carey
IT'S BETTER TO BE OVER THE HILL–
THAN UNDER IT...$5.95
by Jan King
THE PEOPLE WATCHER'S FIELD GUIDE.........$5.95
by R. S. Bean
THE GUILT BAG (Accessory Item) $6.95
by Maxine Schur & Linda Rogers
HOW TO REALLY PARTY $5.95
by Kenyata Sullivan
THE ABSOLUTE **LAST CHANGE** DIET BOOK ..$5.95
by John Kolness and Tim Halle
HUSBANDS FROM HELL $5.95
by Jan King
HORMONES FROM HELL (The Ultimate
Women's Humor Book!)..............................$5.95
by Jan King
FOR **MEN** ONLY (How To Survive Marriage) $5.95
by Evan Keliher
THE Unofficial WOMEN'S DIVORCE GUIDE.....$5.95
by Mary Beth Shank & Suzanne Tumy

HOW TO TALK YOUR WAY OUT OF
   A TRAFFIC TICKET.......................................$4.95
   by David Kelley
WHAT DO WE DO NOW?? (The Complete
   Guide For All New Parents) $4.95
   by Paul Feinsinger

— COMING SOON —

THE CAT OWNER'S SHAPE UP MANUAL
   by Richard Porteus
YOU KNOW YOU'RE AN OLD FART WHEN...
   by Dusty Rumsey
RED HOT MONOGAMY (In Just 60 Seconds A Day)
   by Dr. Patrick Hunt
SHARING THE ROAD WITH IDIOTS
   by Bob Glickman
THE GREATEST ANSWERING MACHINE MESSAGES
   OF ALL TIME
   by John Carfi & Cliff Carle
EVERYTHING YOU ALWAYS WANTED TO KNOW
   ABOUT EVERYTHING
   by Fred Sahner

— BEST SELLERS—

NO HANG-UPS (Funny Answering
   Machine Messages) $3.95
   by John Carfi & Cliff Carle
NO HANG-UPS II $3.95
   by Cliff Carle
NO HANG-UPS III $3.95
   by John Carfi & Cliff Carle
GETTING EVEN WITH
   THE ANSWERING MACHINE.......................$3.95
   by John Carfi & Cliff Carle

THE SUPERIOR PERSON'S GUIDE TO
    EVERYDAY IRRITATIONS $4.95
    by Russ Lindway
YOUR GUIDE TO CORPORATE SURVIVAL $4.95
    by Scott Choate
GIFTING RIGHT (How To Give A Great Gift
    On Any Budget!) $4.95
    by Leslie Sorg
HOW TO GET EVEN WITH YOUR EXes $3.95
    by Marsha Posner Williams & Mike Price
HOW TO SUCCEED IN SINGLES BARS............$3.95
    by Cathi Chamberlain
TOTALLY OUTRAGEOUS
    BUMPER-SNICKERS....................................$2.95
    by Eager Allan Poe, Mark Not-Twain, Kent Clark
THE "MAGIC BOOKMARK" BOOK COVER
    (Accessory Item)..$2.95

— CASSETTES —

NO HANG-UPS TAPES $4.98
    by John Carfi & Cliff Carle
    (Funny, Pre-recorded Answering Machine
    Messages With Hilarious Sound Effects) —
    In Male or Female Voices
Vol. I: GENERAL MESSAGES
Vol II: BUSINESS MESSAGES
Vol III: 'R' RATED MESSAGES
Vol IV: SOUND EFFECTS ONLY
Vol V: CELEBRI-TEASE (Celebrity Impersonations)